An I Can Read Book®

PROVE IT!

by Rose Wyler
and Gerald Ames
Pictures by
Tālivaldis Stubis
Harper & Row
Publishers

CONTENTS

When something is true,
you can prove it.

Do you know—
  Water is dry—sometimes?
  Air can stretch?
  You can hear with your teeth?
  A magnet will pull through your finger?

These things are true.
Try them! Do experiments.
This book tells you how.

EXPERIMENTS
WITH WATER

WHY DROPS ARE ROUND

You will need:

a piece of wax paper

soap

an eye dropper

water

Fill the eye dropper with water.

Drip some drops on the wax paper.

See how round they are!

The outside of a drop is like a skin.

It holds the drop together.

Now take a little piece of soap
and wet the end.

Touch a drop of water.

The skin breaks—
the drop spreads out.

MAKE A NEEDLE FLOAT

Fill a dish with water.
Take a needle
and a fork.
Put the needle on the fork.

Hold the fork near the water.
Let the needle roll into the water.
The needle floats!
It makes a dent on the water.

The top of the water is like a skin.

It holds the needle up.

Push the needle down.

The skin breaks, and the needle sinks.

Some bugs can walk on water.

The skin holds them up.

Their legs dent the water.

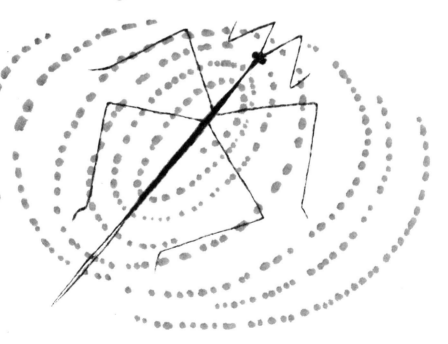

CHASE THE PEPPER

Fill a pie plate with water.
Shake pepper on the water.
Then take a piece of wet soap
and dip it into the water.
See the pepper run!
It runs from the soapy water
to the clear water.
Why?

The skin on water pulls.
On soapy water the pull is weak.
On clear water it is strong.
The clear water pulls the pepper along.

Now take some sugar
and shake it into the soapy water.
The pepper runs back!
Sugar gives the skin a stronger pull.

A BOAT THAT RUNS WITH SOAP

Take a piece of aluminum foil
and make a little boat.
Cut a piece of soap—like this.
Put the soap on the boat.

Float the boat
and away it goes.
It goes from soapy water
to clear water.
You know why.
The clear water has a stronger pull.
You proved it!

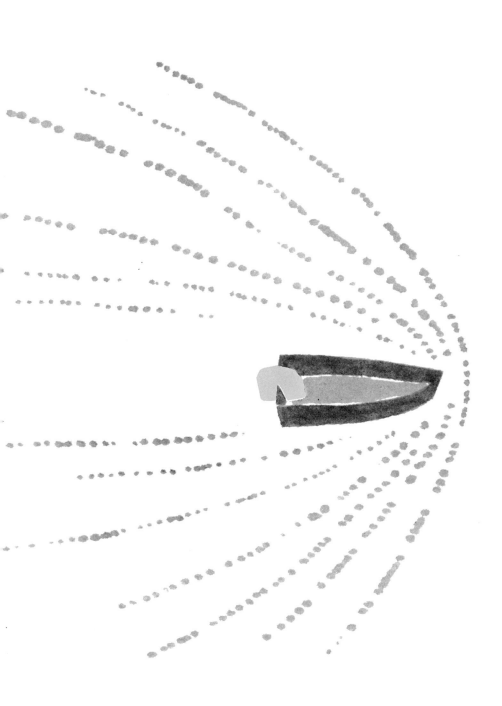

WETTER WATER

Water is wet,

but you can make it wetter.

Cut out two little men from newspaper.

Take two glasses.
Put clear water in one glass
and soapy water in the other.
Hold a paper man over each glass.
Drop them in.
Both men get wet. They start to sink.
The man in the soapy water gets wet first
and sinks first. Why?
The soapy water
wets him faster.
It is wetter water.

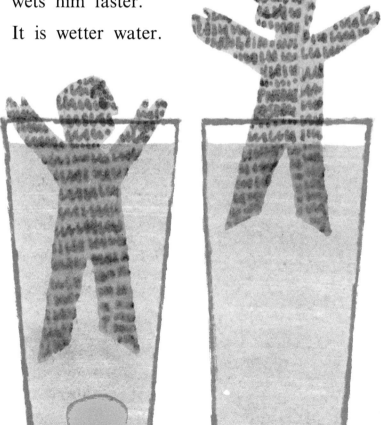

IS WATER ALWAYS WET?

No. Not always.
When water turns to ice,
it is dry.
Prove it!
Take a piece of paper.
Open the freezer.
Touch an ice cube with the paper.
The paper stays dry because—
the ice is dry.

When you fall on ice,
you do not get wet.
Ice is dry water.

WATER YOU CANNOT SEE

Plop! Splash!

Down you go into a puddle.

Your coat is wet.

You hang it up and it dries.

Where does the water go?

18

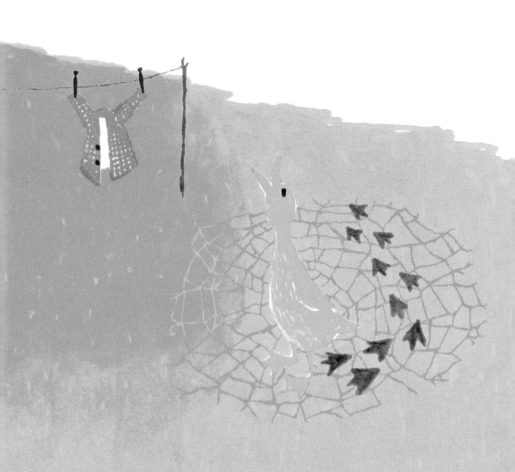

The water goes into the air.

It turns into a dry gas.

You cannot see this gas,

but it is in the air.

The puddle will dry up, too,

and the water will go into the air.

YOU CAN GET WATER FROM AIR

Prove it!
Take a jar.
Be sure the outside is dry.
Fill the jar with ice,
then put the cover on.

Soon you will see
little drops of water on the jar.
Where do they come from?
From inside the jar?
Oh, no! They come from the air outside.
The air has water in it
that you cannot see.
This water turns into drops
when the air around the jar cools off.

COLD WATER IS HEAVY

You can prove it.
Take a glass bowl
and fill it with warm water.
Take a small bottle
and fill it with cold water.
Color the cold water.

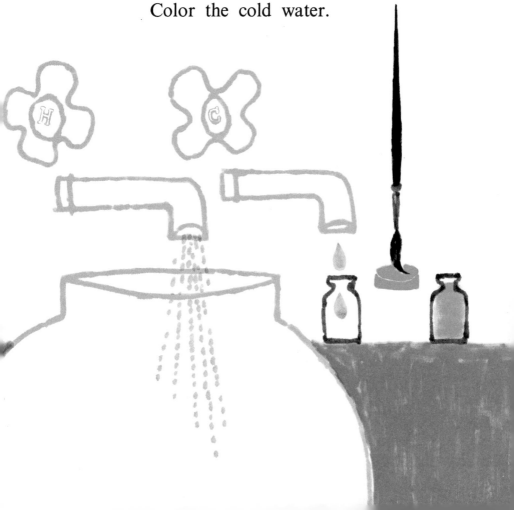

Pick up the bottle.

Put your thumb on its mouth.

Hold the bottle sideways

and lower it into the warm water.

Take away your thumb.

Look! The cold water sinks.

It is heavy—

heavier than the warm water.

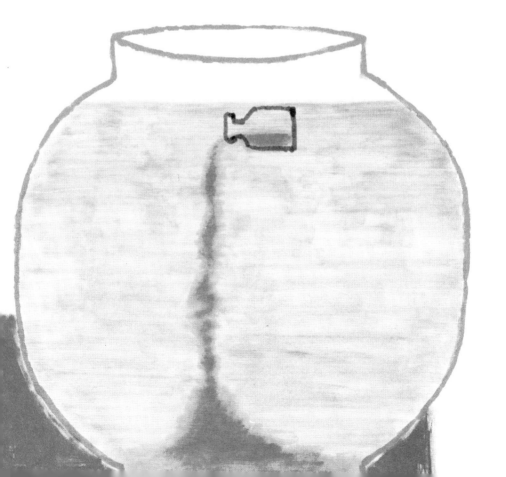

Now fill the bowl with cold water.
Fill the bottle with warm water
and color the water.
Hold your thumb
on the mouth of the bottle
and lower it
to the bottom of the bowl.
Set it down on its side
and take away your thumb.
The warm water rises.
You know why.
It is lighter than the cold water.

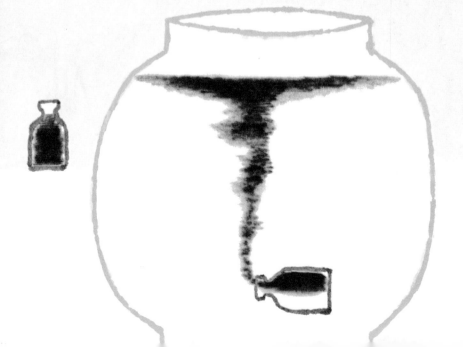

EXPERIMENTS WITH AIR

BLOW DOWN A BIG BOOK

Take a paper bag
and make
a neck in it—
like this.

Stand a big book on the bag.

Hold the neck
and blow air into the bag.
The air fills the bag.
The air pushes on the book.
Bang!
Down it goes.

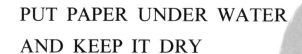

PUT PAPER UNDER WATER
AND KEEP IT DRY

Stuff paper into a glass.
Turn the glass upside down
and lower it under water.

Now lift up the glass.

Feel the paper—it is dry!

Why?

There is air in the glass.

The air keeps the water out.

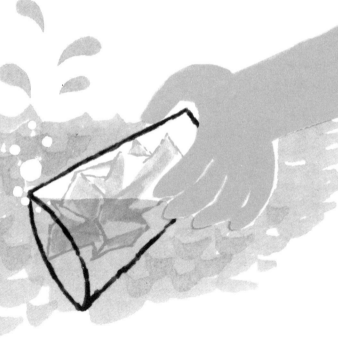

You can get the air out of the glass.

Lower it under water again, then tilt it.

The air goes out, water goes in,

and the paper gets wet.

PICK UP PAPER WITHOUT TOUCHING IT

Take a paper cup
and make a hole in the bottom.
Put a sheet of paper on a table.
Set the cup on it
with the bottom up.
Suck through the hole
and lift the cup.
Up comes the paper!

What holds the paper up?
Air.
Air presses all around.
It presses up, it presses down.

When you suck air from the cup,
the pressure inside is weak.
The pressure outside is stronger.
Air presses under the paper
and holds it up.

AIR CAN LIFT WATER

Prove it!
Fill a soda bottle with water
and put a straw in it.
Take some clay
and stick it around the straw.
Suck on the straw.
Does the water come up? No.
What is wrong?
The clay keeps air
away from the water.

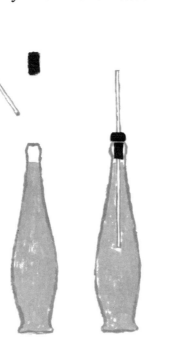

Now take the clay away and suck.

Up comes the water.

Why?

Because air presses down on the water
and helps push it up the straw.

THE TALL, TALL STRAW

Air will lift water very high.
You can prove it.
Take two straws
and put them together
like this.

Tape them with sticky tape.
Now you have a tall straw.
Suck on the straw.
Up comes the water.

Tape three straws together,
then four.
Suck through the straws.
See how high the water will go.

35

YOU CAN *NOT* EMPTY A BOX

For your box, use a milk carton.
The carton looks empty,
but it is full—full of air.

Hold the open end near your face.
Squeeze it
and feel the air blow out.

Now try this.

Put bits of paper on a table.

Hold the carton near them.

Squeeze the carton

and see what happens.

Air blows the paper away.

YOU CAN STRETCH AIR

You will need:
a can with a small mouth
a balloon
a toaster

Be sure the can has nothing in it but air.
Put the balloon over the mouth.
Set the can on the toaster
and heat it.

38

Soon the balloon blows up.
Why?
The air in the can gets hot.
This makes the air stretch.
The air takes up more room
and blows up the balloon.

Now put a pot holder around the can
and pick up the can.
Be careful—it is hot.
Put the can in the refrigerator.
Look—the balloon goes down.
As the air cools off, it shrinks.

EXPERIMENTS WITH SOUND

MAKE A RULER SING

You need a thin ruler
made of wood or plastic or metal.
Hold the ruler on a table—like this.

Bend it down, then let it go.
Listen to the ruler.
It hums!
It sings!

What makes the ruler sing?
It shakes up and down—it VIBRATES.
When the ruler vibrates, it hums.
When it stops vibrating,
the song ends.

YOU CAN FEEL SOUND

Blow up a balloon.

Pinch the neck and stretch it a little.

Let some air out and the balloon cries.

The neck vibrates.

You can see it. You can feel it.

The air vibrates, too.

This makes the sound.

You can feel your own voice.
Put your fingers on your throat
and say "Hello."
Feel the vibration.
All sounds are vibrations.

SOUND GOES THROUGH THE AIR

Your friend says "Hi!"
He makes the air vibrate.
The vibrations move from him to you
and you hear him.

46

SOUND GOES THROUGH
THE GROUND

You can hear a friend another way.
You put your ear to the ground.
She jumps around
and you hear her footsteps.
The Indians did this, too,
to hear footsteps.

SOUND GOES THROUGH WOOD

You can prove it.
Ask your friend to take a watch
and hold it on one end of a long ruler.
Put the other end to your ear.
Tick-tick, tick-tick.
The sound goes through the wood.

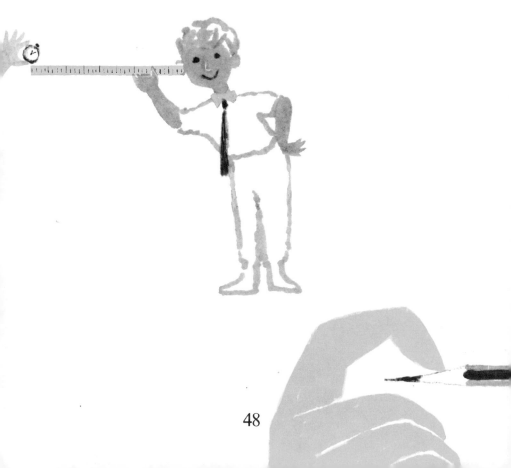

YOU CAN HEAR WITH YOUR TEETH

Take a pencil
and hold one end between your teeth.
Scratch the other end.
Hear the scratching!
Vibrations go through the wood
and through your teeth.

A JAR OF NOISE

Hold a jar near your ear.
What a noise!
What a roar!
Where does the noise come from?
There are little sounds in the air
all around you.
The sounds make the air
in the jar vibrate
and you hear them.

Fill the jar with water,
so there is no air in it.
Now listen. What do you hear?
Nothing.

Listen to a big seashell.
The shell is noisy, too.
It makes a sound
like the roar of the sea.
It catches sounds from the air.
If you fill the shell with water,
will it still roar?

EXPERIMENTS WITH MAGNETS

TEST YOUR MAGNET

Is your magnet strong?
Test it with paper clips.
They are made of steel.
The magnet will pick them up.

One clip, two clips, three clips.
Hang them end to end.
How many will your magnet hold?

MAKE A MAGNET

Take a paper clip and open it—
Straighten it out.
Now it is just a steel wire.

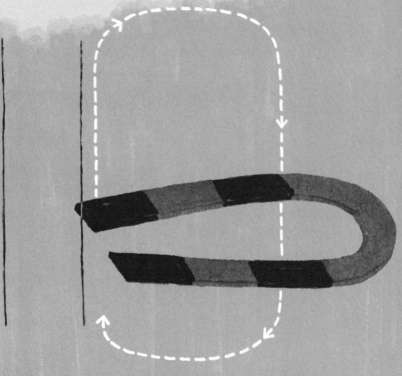

Rub the wire with one end of your magnet.
Rub the wire 20 times.
Always go the same way.
Do not go back and forth.

Now test the wire.
Take some steel wool
and pull it to bits.
Does the wire pick up the bits?
It does! The wire is a magnet.

MANY MAGNETS FROM ONE

Cut your wire magnet
into two pieces.
Cut the two pieces
into smaller pieces.
All are magnets.
You can prove it!
Test the pieces with steel wool.
All pick up steel wool.
All are magnets.

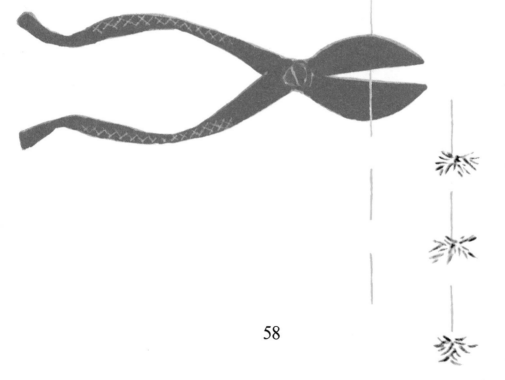

MAKE A NEEDLE STAND IN THE AIR

Thread a needle.
Tie the thread around a book
and put the needle on top.

Lift the needle with a magnet.
Make it point straight up.

Slowly lift the magnet
above the needle.
Look! The needle stands in the air!

A MAGNET WILL PULL
THROUGH YOUR FINGER

Hold a paper clip
between your finger and thumb.
Then hold a magnet
on top of your finger.

Move your thumb away —
the clip hangs from your finger!

A magnet pulls through other things, too.
It pulls through paper, glass, wood.
Try it! Prove it!

MAGNETIC PUPPETS

A shoe box can be your stage.
Use a paper cup for a house.
Set it on the stage.

Cut out puppets from paper.
Cut out a man and a dog.
Put paper clips on their feet
and stand them on the stage.

To move a puppet,
move a magnet under the stage.
Make the man chase the dog
into the house.
Then make the dog chase the man.
At the end of the show,
have them be friends.

After the show, save the puppets.

Keep them in the box with the magnet.

Keep things from other experiments, too.

You will use them again.